Watch Out!

CONTENTS

NATIONAL GEOGRAPHIC

School Publishing

Hampton-Brown

Words with **al**, **all**

Look at each picture. Read the words.

al_
all

Example:

w**al**nuts

h**all**

t**all**

sm**all**

c**all**

w**al**rus

2

Key Words

Look at the pictures. Read the sentences.

Bird-Watching

1. Baby birds **cry** as if **hurt**, but they're just saying, "More food, **please**!"
2. These birds **jump** on a hippo and **ride** around on the water.
3. This bird swims **close** to **green** **plants**, looking for fish.
4. This bird **shows** off its feathers while this bird **sleeps**.

What does a duck do to help it sleep?

Phonics Games

NGReach.com

3

Bird Partners

by Jamie Rowley

giraffe

In the animal world, birds often partner with mammals. The mammals' coat or hide is filled with bugs that birds eat. Sitting on mammals, the birds can eat as much as they please.

rhino

elk

capybara

Giraffes, rhinos, and elk may have bird partners. Capybaras have bird partners, too. A capybara is a mammal, like these other animals. It stands about 18 inches tall and has soft, dark fur.

The capybara has a big head and stumpy tail. It looks a lot like a big hamster. It lives in marshes, ponds, and rivers where birds also live.

A capybara spends almost all its life in the water or very close to water. It can stay underwater like a hippo, so that just its eyes, ears, and nose show.

This soggy hiding place keeps the capybara
safe from wild dogs and cats, snakes, and other
land animals that want to eat it.

When it is moving, the capybara wades in
the water close to the shore. There, it can eat all
the green plants it pleases.

A bird that partners with a capybara picks small bugs from the mammal's fur. The bird picks at scabs and cuts. This does not seem to hurt the capybara at all. It can even sleep while it gets groomed.

turkey vulture

tick bird

A capybara will be close partners with any bird that it pleases. Such birds include small tick birds and big black turkey vultures.

Birds that partner with a capybara will stick close to their partner. They will ride on the capybara's head as it swims. These birds will ride on its back as it splashes in and out of the water.

A capybara in danger will cry out with a gruff bark as a warning. A partner bird will jump up and follow. Its sharp calls and flapping wings help scare off enemies.

If you're ever exploring on the banks of the Amazon River, watch for a bird that seems to be standing on the top of the water. If you take a close look, you may also see the shiny eyes of the capybara staring back at you. ❖

Words with <u>al</u>, <u>all</u>

Read these words.

mall	walnut	store	wallet	bowl
bill	walrus	small	bald	salt

Find the words with **al** or **all**.
Use letters to build them.

m a l l

Talk Together

Tell your partner what
to look for.

Find a _store_ in
the _mall_.

Words with <u>oi</u>, <u>oy</u>

Look at each picture. Read the words.

oi
_oy

Example:

t**oy**

r**oy**al

s**oi**l

p**oi**nt

n**oi**sy

enj**oy**

High Frequency
Words

close
cry
green
hurt
jump
plant
please
ride
show
sleep

Key Words

Look at the pictures. Read the sentences.

Killer Whale Facts

1. Killer whales **ride** the waves **close** together in a pod, which is a group name and not a **green** pea **plant**!

2. Studies **show** that a killer whale may **sleep** by resting half of its brain at a time.

3. Killer whales can sing, **cry**, squeak, and creak as loud and long as they **please**.

4. When killer whales breach, they **jump** out of the water and crash down, but it does not **hurt** them.

Why do you think killer whales jump out of the water?

Phonics Games
NGReach.com

17

Sea Voyage

by Jane Kincaid

People enjoy spending time by the sea. They relax and loiter, soaking up the hot sun. Then they jump in and swim to cool down.

sea bird

fish

grass

Plants and animals like these moist habitats, too. Sea birds cry out when they spot fish to eat. Tall green grass grows in nearby dunes.

But some forms of life spend all their time in the water. Their home is the royal-blue sea.

Life in the deep sea is not like life on land. Many of the animals that live under the water never sleep. Most fish are always swimming. They have no choice but to swim or sink!

The remora is not like most fish. A remora has another way to get around. It latches on to something bigger and faster.

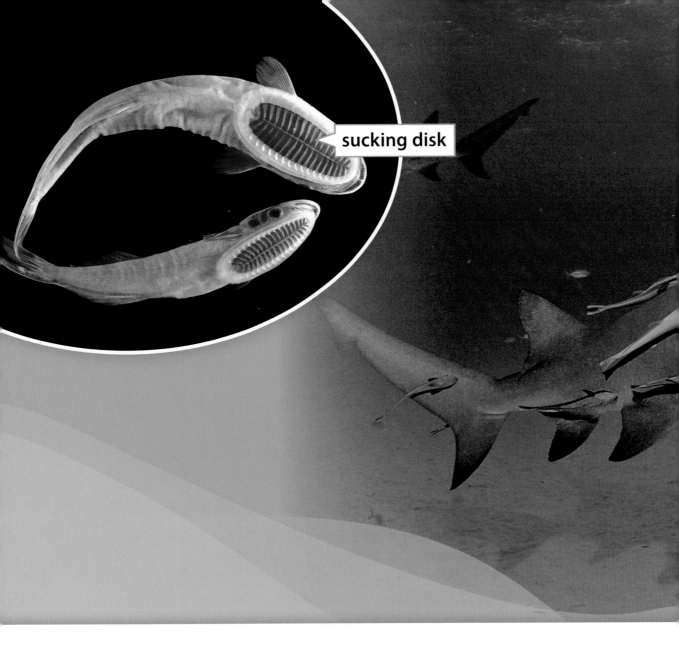

sucking disk

The remora is a short, chunky fish. It has a sucking disk on the top of its long, flat head. It uses this disk to latch on to the body of other animals.

Once the remora has joined itself to a whale, shark, or sea turtle, it just hangs on. It rides along while its host swims about as it pleases.

The remora can't survive in still water. It needs to keep water rushing past its gills. So it joins up with an animal that keeps moving all the time, doing the swimming for both of them.

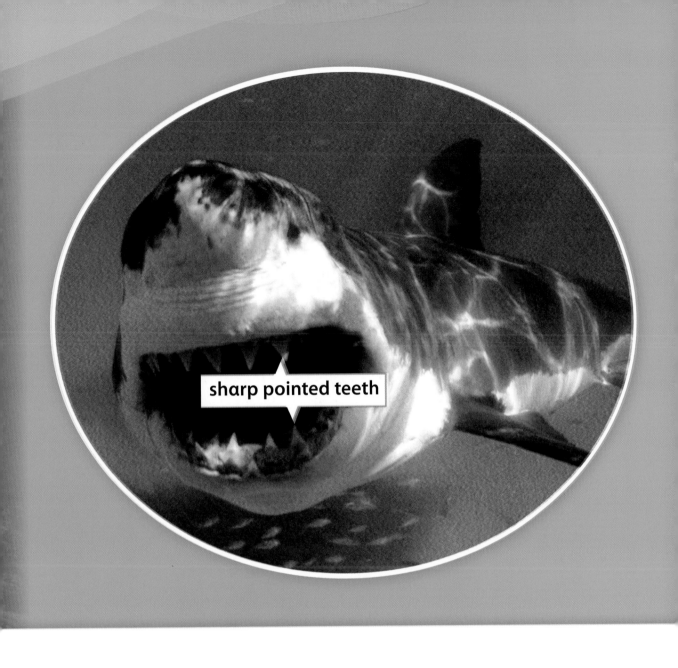

sharp pointed teeth

If fish had a choice, almost all of them would steer clear of sharks. A shark's sharp, pointed teeth mean death to almost any living thing in its path. But not the remora. No dead remora has ever been found inside a shark.

whale

remora

The remora can use its host to provide food and a safe hiding place. Sharks, whales, and other deep-sea hosts don't try to hurt the remora. They also don't seem to care if they have a remora stuck to them.

Studies show that the remora can leave its host whenever it pleases. It leaves in order to eat. In doing so, it may be a helpful partner. It stays close by and acts as a cleaner. It feeds on organisms that may hurt its host.

Yes, the remora helps the shark, but it gets the better deal. Because of the shark, the remora enjoys a wide range of food and a safe hiding place. When it comes to finding a smart way to live, the remora really uses its head! ❖

Words with <u>oi</u>, <u>oy</u>

Read these words.

moist	voice	playful	seals	choice
enjoys	joyful	boy	soil	noisy

Find the words with **oi** or **oy**. Use letters to build them.

c h o i c e

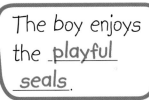

Talk Together

Choose words from the box above to tell your partner what the boy likes to do by the sea.

> The boy enjoys the _playful_ _seals_.

Make Your Choice

Play with a partner. Answer each question below. Then tell why you made that choice. Now it's your partner's turn.

1 Which food comes from a plant—a crunchy walnut or a boiled egg?

2 Which would you enjoy more—to sleep by a waterfall or to ride on a horse?

3 Which gift would please a small boy more—a soft toy bear or a toy truck?

4 Which makes more noise—kids in the hall or a small green frog?

5 Which would you want in your wallet—a coin or a bill?

6 Which voice do you enjoy more—a bird calling or a dog barking?

Acknowledgments

Grateful acknowledgment is given to the authors, artists, photographers, museums, publishers, and agents for permission to reprint copyrighted material. Every effort has been made to secure the appropriate permission. If any omissions have been made or if corrections are required, please contact the Publisher.

Photographic Credits

CVR Masa Ushioda/WaterFrame - Underwater Images/Photolibrary. **2** (bl) Rolf Bruderer/Blend Images/Corbis. (br) Nick Norman/National Geographic Image Collection. (c) Wolfgang Kaehler/Alamy Images. (tl) PhotoDisc/Getty Images. (tr) New England Pix/Alamy Images. **3** (b) Liz Garza Williams/ Hampton-Brown/National Geographic School Publishing. (cl) Gerry Ellis/Minden Pictures/National Geographic Image Collection. (cr) James M. Wedge/VIREO, The Academy of Natural Sciences. (tl) Cheryl E. Davis/Shutterstock. (tr) archana bhartia/Shutterstock. **4** (inset) Cyril Russo/JH Editorial/ Minden Pictures/National Geographic Image Collection. **4-5** (tc) Caroline Webber/age fotostock/ Photolibrary. **5** (cr) Konrad Wothe/Minden Pictures/National Geographic Image Collection. (tr) Joel Sartore/National Geographic Image Collection. **6** Ross Wallace/Shutterstock. **7** Prisma/ SuperStock. **8** (cl) Andrew Moss/Adams Picture Library t/a apl/Alamy Images. (cr) Ingo Arndt/ Minden Pictures/National Geographic Image Collection. (tl) Jennifer Hollman/National Geographic Image Collection. **9** John Waters/Minden Pictures. **10-11** (t) Dave and Sigrun Tollerton/Alamy Images. **11** (cr) Gary Martin/iStockphoto. (tl) Denis Blofield/Shutterstock. **12-13** Top-Pics TBK/ Alamy Images. **14** SuperStock RF/SuperStock. **15** (bc) Barbara J. Petrick/Shutterstock. (bl) Sherwin McGehee/iStockphoto. (br) Elena Schweitzer/Shutterstock. (cr) Liz Garza Williams/Hampton-Brown/ National Geographic School Publishing. **16** (bl) Laurence Griffiths/Getty Images. (br) Gary Conner/ PhotoEdit. (cl) Organics image library/Alamy Images. (cr) George Doyle/Stockdisc/Getty Images. (tl) Stockbyte/Getty Images. (tr) Scala/White Images/Art Resource, Inc. **17** (b) Liz Garza Williams/ Hampton-Brown/National Geographic School Publishing. (tl) Alaska Stock Images/age fotostock. (tr) Jay Schlegel/Photographer's Choice/Getty Images. **18-19** (t) John Lamb/Getty Images. **19** (c) Marko Heuver/Shutterstock. (tl) anacarol/Shutterstock. **21** (t) Norbert Wu/Minden Pictures. **22** (tl) Norbert Wu/Minden Pictures/National Geographic Image Collection. **22-23** (t) Reinhard Dirscherl/ Visuals Unlimited/Getty Images. **24** Fred Bavendam/Minden Pictures/National Geographic Image Collection. **25** Paul Sutherland/National Geographic Image Collection. **26-27** (t) Flip Nicklin/Minden Pictures/National Geographic Image Collection. **27** Norbert Wu/Minden Pictures. **28** Brian J. Skerry/ National Geographic/Getty Images. **29** Liz Garza Williams/Hampton-Brown/National Geographic School Publishing. **30** (bl) Picsfive/Shutterstock. (br) D. Hurst/Alamy Images. (cl) Mike Theiss/ National Geographic Image Collection. (cr) Phovoir/FCM Graphic/Alamy Images. (tl) John Foxx Images/ Imagestate. (tr) Torsten Stahlberg/iStockphoto. **31** (bl) Steve Byland/iStockphoto. (br) Konrad Wothe/ imagebroker/Alamy Images. (cl) Image Club. (cr) Ilene MacDonald/Alamy. (tl) Fancy/Veer/Corbis. (tr) Creatas/Jupiterimages. **20-21** (t) image100/SuperStock.

Illustrator Credits

17, **29** Aga Kowalski

The National Geographic Society

John M. Fahey, Jr., President & Chief Executive Officer
Gilbert M. Grosvenor, Chairman of the Board

National Geographic School Publishing
Hampton-Brown
www.NGSP.com

Printed in the USA.
RR Donnelley, Jefferson City, MO

ISBN: 978-0-7362-8082-2

12 13 14 15 16 17 18 19
10 9 8 7 6 5 4